Alfred's Basic Piano Library

Prep Course

FOR THE YOUNG BEGINNER

Notespeller Book

Level D

Students who read fluently will be able to enjoy playing the piano for a lifetime. The activities in this NOTESPELLER BOOK aid students in developing reading skills and recognizing interval and chord patterns. Concepts are reinforced through games, puzzles, coloring pages and written exercises. Students are encouraged to play many of the notated examples to further enhance the reading process. This book provides an enjoyable and appealing way to have fun while learning valuable musical skills!

Instructions for Use

1. This NOTESPELLER is designed to be used with Alfred's PREP COURSE for the young beginner, LESSON BOOK D. It can also serve as an effective supplement for other piano methods.

2. This book is coordinated page-by-page with the LESSON BOOK, and assignments are ideally made according to the instructions in the upper right corner of each page of the NOTESPELLER.

D1416130

Gayle Kowalchyk • E. L. Lancaster

Cover illustration and interior art by Christine Finn

Measuring Intervals
(Down)

1. Draw a half note DOWN from the given note in each measure to make the indicated melodic interval. Turn the stems UP for notes below the third line; turn the stems DOWN for notes on or above the third line.

Up-stem   Down-stem

2. Write the name of each note in the square below it.

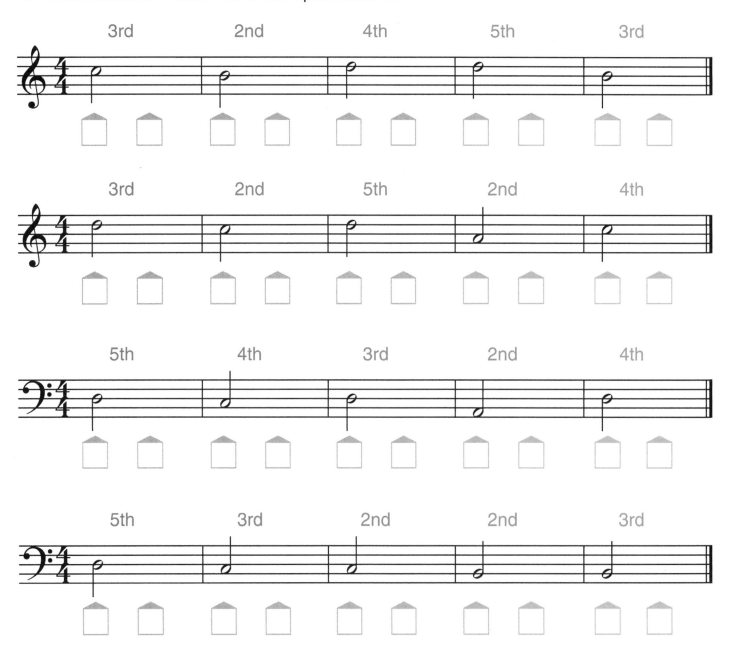

Name the Notes
(Harmonic Intervals)

1. Draw a whole note BELOW the given note to make the indicated harmonic interval.

2. Write the names of the notes in the squares below the staff. Write the name of the lower note in the lower square, the name of the higher note in the higher square.

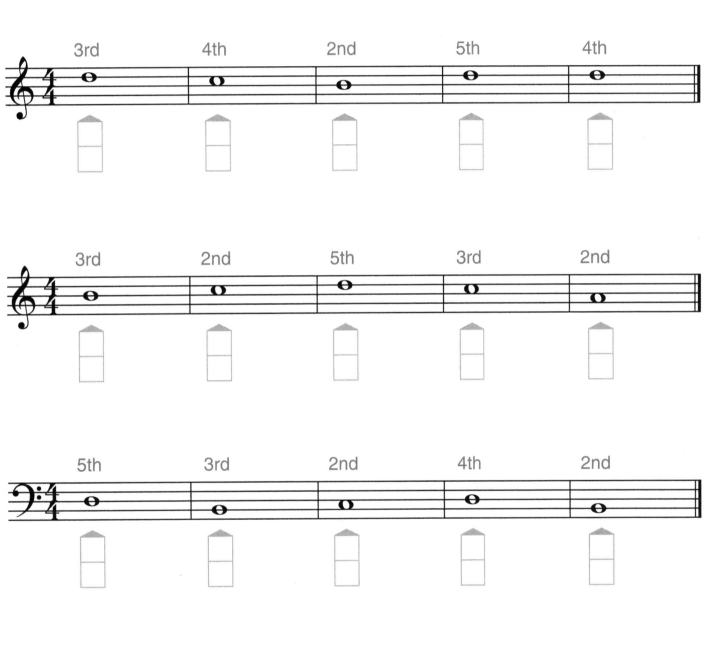

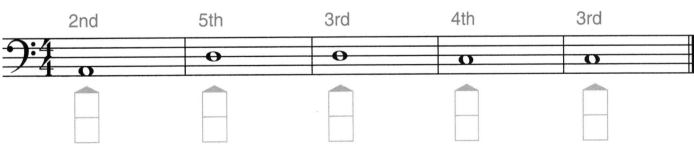

Use with page 7.

Complete the Picture
(G Position Review)

G Position

1. Color the areas containing a G **green**.
2. Color the areas containing an A **yellow**.
3. Color the areas containing a B **orange**.
4. Color the areas containing a C **blue**.
5. Color the areas containing a D **purple**.

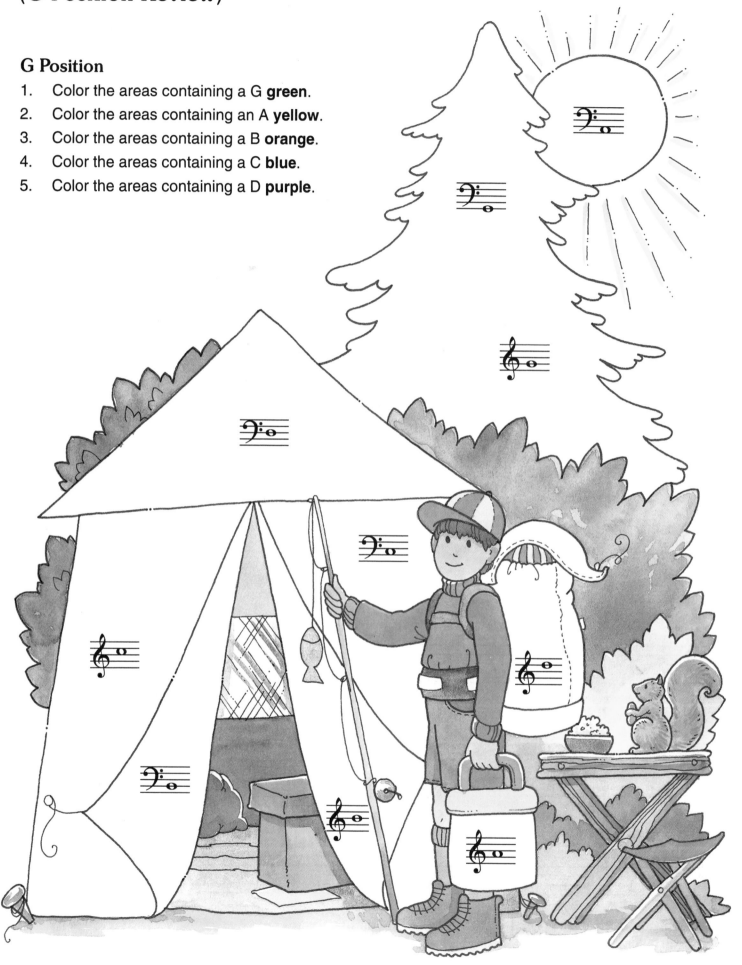

Writing G Position with LH an Octave Higher

1. Write the LH notes of the NEW G POSITION in the BASS staff under the squares. Use QUARTER NOTES. Turn all the stems DOWN.

2. Write the RH notes in the TREBLE staff over the squares. Use QUARTER NOTES. Turn the stems of G and A UP. Turn the stems of B, C, and D DOWN.

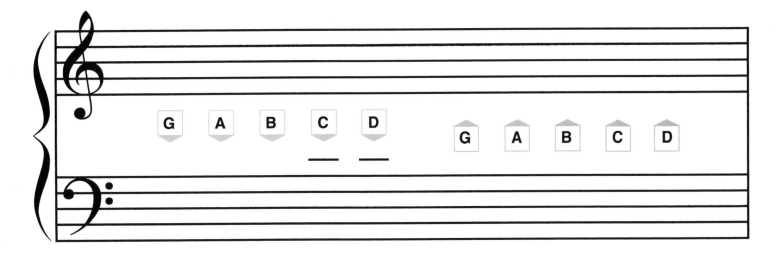

3. Write the name of each note in the square below it. The letters in each group of squares will spell a familiar word. Play and say the note names.

Use with page 9.

Name the Notes

Write the name of each note in the square below it,
then play and say the note names.

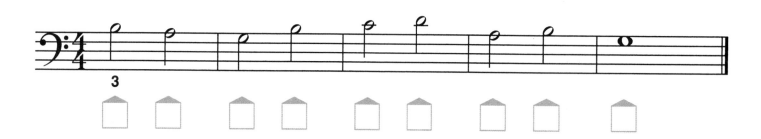

New G Position

1. Print the letter names for both the left hand and right hand G POSITION with LH an OCTAVE HIGHER on the keyboard below.

2. Draw a line to connect each note on the staff to the appropriate key on the keyboard.

3. In the exercise below, write the names of the notes in the squares above the staff. Write the name of the lower note in the lower square, the name of the higher note in the higher square.

4. Write the names of the HARMONIC INTERVALS in the boxes below the staff.

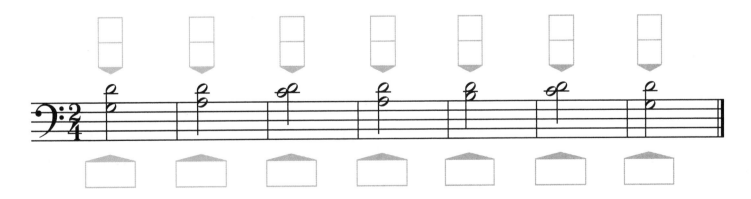

Use with page 12.

Connect-the-Dots Puzzle
(New G Position)

Draw lines connecting the dots on the matching boxes.

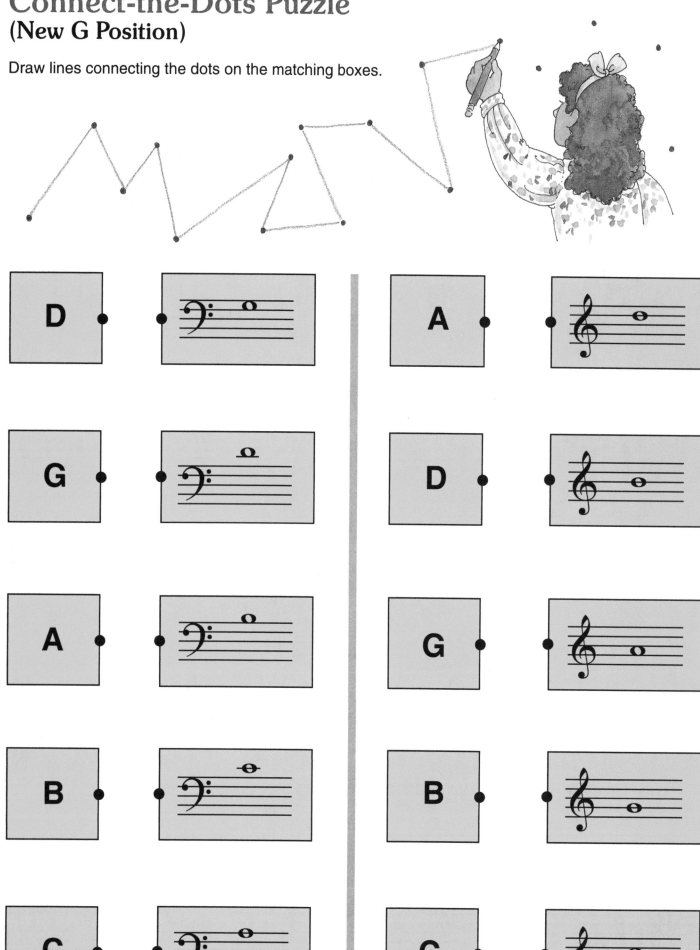

The Case of the Missing Notes
(C Position and New G Position with LH an Octave Higher)

1. Write the missing notes on the staff from the C POSITION and G POSITION with LH an OCTAVE HIGHER. Use whole notes.

2. Write the name of each note in the square below it.

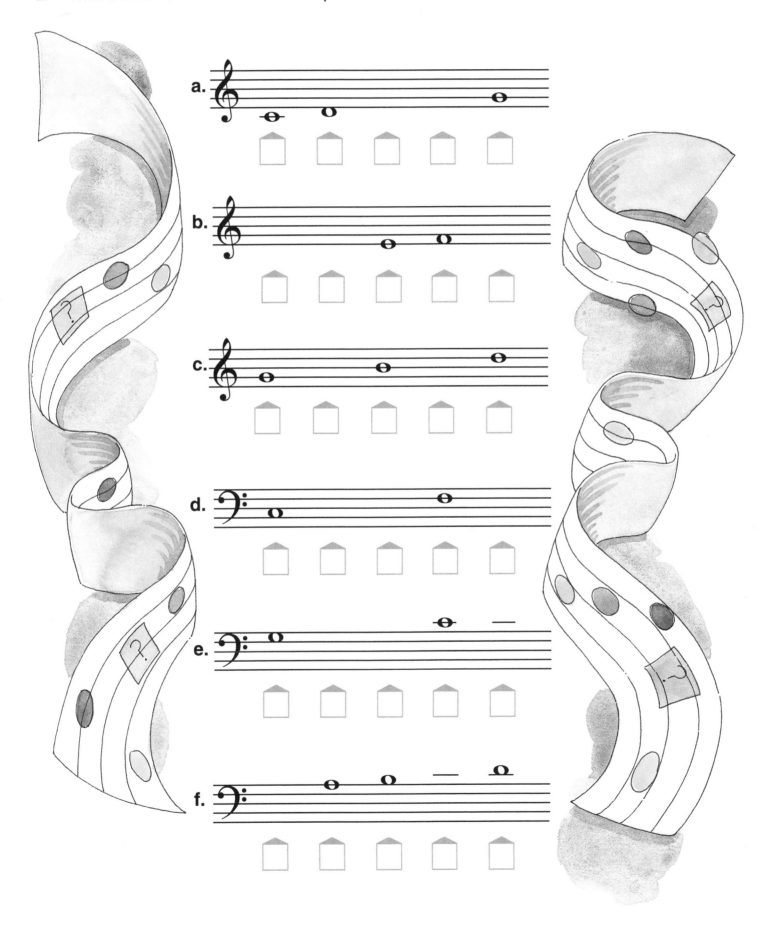

Eighth Note Match-Up

Circle the notes that match each group of letters.

Use with pages 14–15.

1 **B C D B**

2. **A B C A**

3. **E F G E**

4. **D C B A**

5. **G F E D**

6. **D C B A**

Interval and Key Matching Game

Draw lines connecting the dots to match the
intervals to their location on the keyboard.

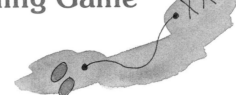

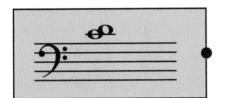
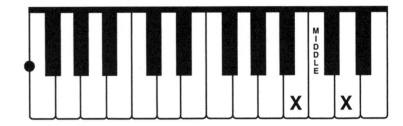

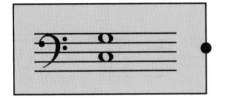
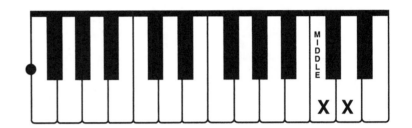

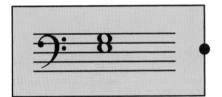
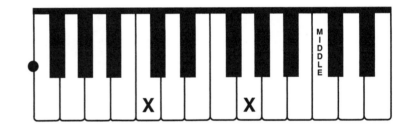

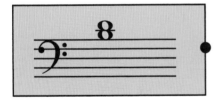
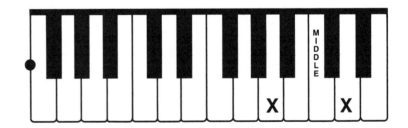

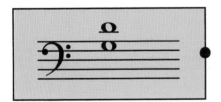
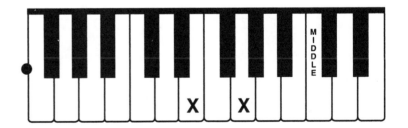

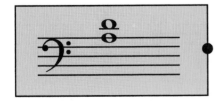
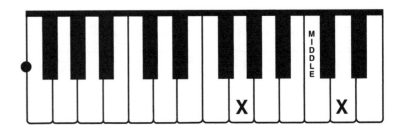

The Case of the Missing Notes
(Four Positions)

Use with page 18.

1. Write the missing notes on the staffs from the given positions.
2. Write the name of each note in the square below it.

D Position

a.

F Position

b.

C Position

c.

E Position

d.

Position and Key Matching Game

Draw lines connecting the dots to match the positions
to their locations on the keyboard.

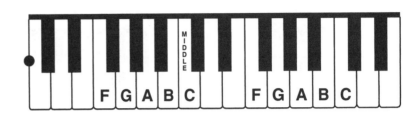

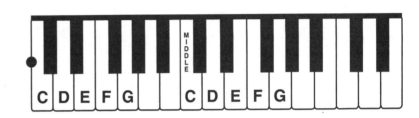

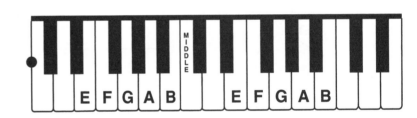

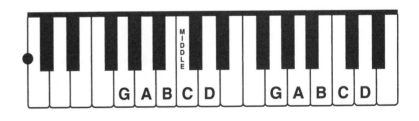

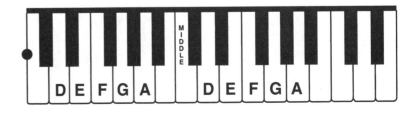

Coloring Fifths

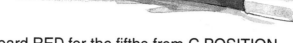

Use with pages 20–21.

1. Color the keys on the keyboard RED for the fifths from C POSITION.

2. Color the keys on the keyboard BLUE for the fifths from F POSITION.

3. Color the keys on the keyboard YELLOW for the fifths from G POSITION.

a.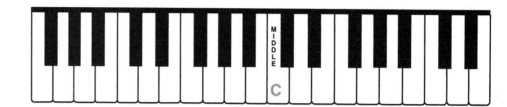

b.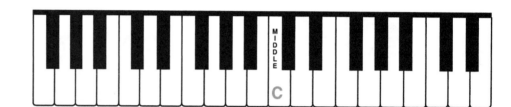

c.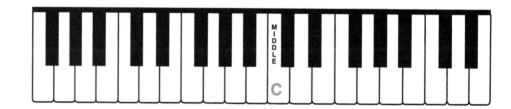

d.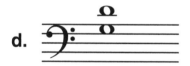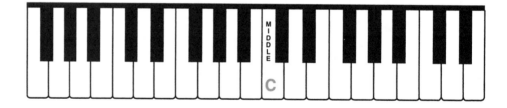

e.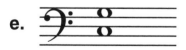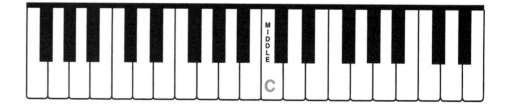

f.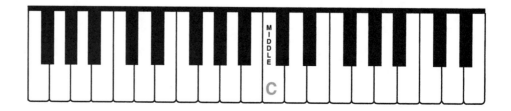

Naming Harmonic Intervals

1. In the exercises below, write the names of the notes in the squares above the staff. Write the name of the lower note in the lower square, the name of the higher note in the higher square.

2. Write the names of the HARMONIC INTERVALS in the boxes below the staff.

Use with pages 24–25.

Naming Melodic Intervals

1. In the exercises below, identify the MELODIC INTERVALS. If the interval moves UP,
   write UP in the higher box; if it moves DOWN, write DOWN in the higher box.
   Write the name of the interval in the lower box.

2. Write the names of the notes in the squares below the staff.

Drawing Half Steps

1. Draw a half note UP from the given note to make a HALF STEP.
    Add a sharp or flat if indicated in the square below. Turn the
    stems UP for notes below the third line. Turn the stems DOWN
    for notes on or above the third line.

Up-stem   Down-stem

2. Write the name of each note in the square below it.

3. Draw a half note DOWN from the given note to make a HALF STEP. Add a sharp or
    natural if indicated in the square below. Turn the stems UP for notes below the third line.
    Turn the stems DOWN for notes on or above the third line.

4. Write the name of each note in the square below it.

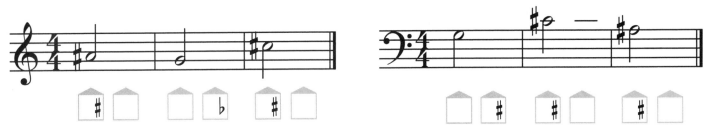

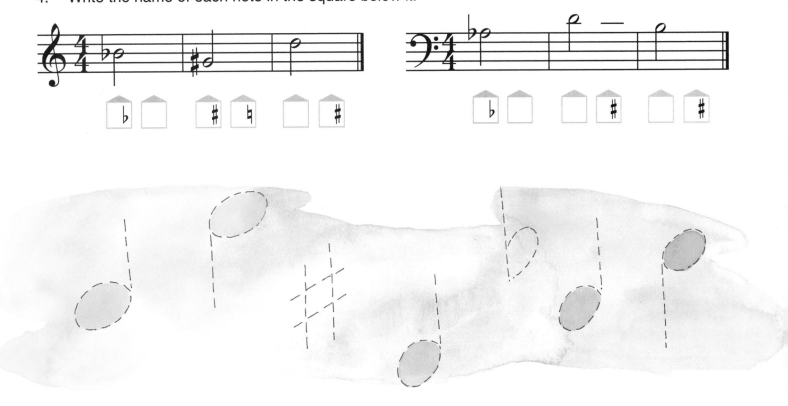

Use with page 27.

Connect-the-Dots Puzzle
(Half Steps)

Draw lines connecting the dots on the matching boxes.

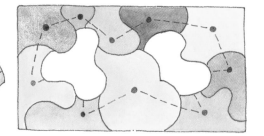

 B-C 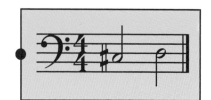   **D♭-C**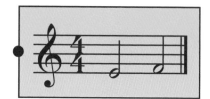

 C♯-D 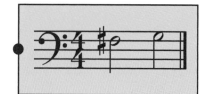   **C-B**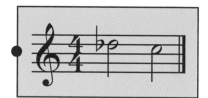

 F♯-G 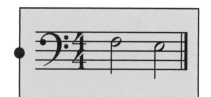   **E-F**

 A♭-G   **E♭-D**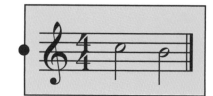

B♭-A 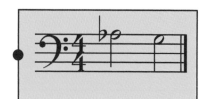   **F♯-G**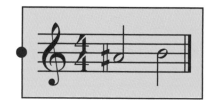

 F-E 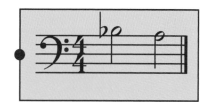   **A♯-B**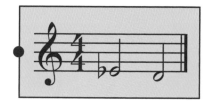

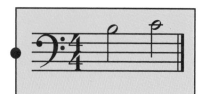

Coloring Half Steps

1. Color the keys on the keyboard GREEN for the half steps going UP.
2. Color the keys on the keyboard RED for the half steps going DOWN.

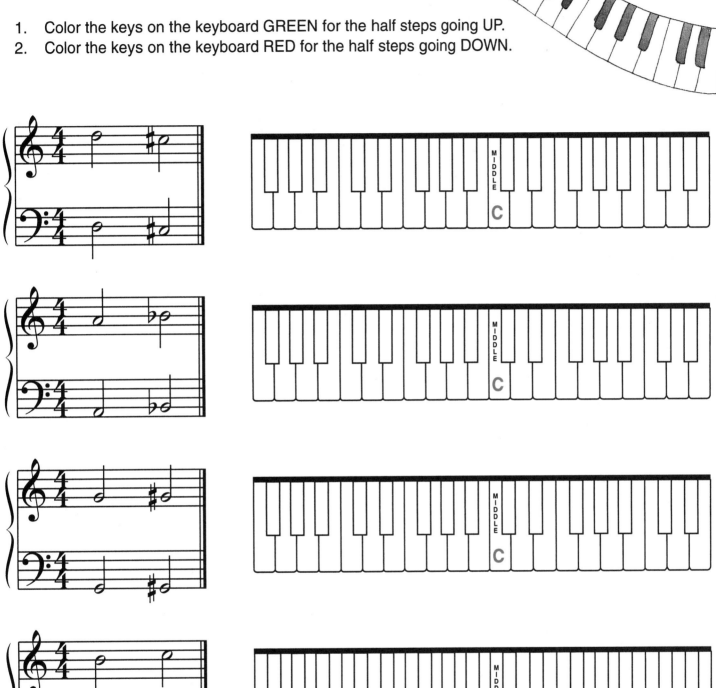

Use with page 30.

Drawing Whole Steps

1. Draw a half note UP from the given note to make a WHOLE STEP. Add a sharp or flat if indicated in the square below. Turn the stems UP in the treble clef, stems DOWN in the bass clef.

2. Write the name of each note in the square below it.

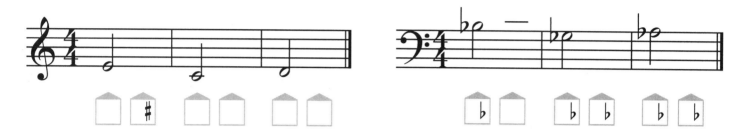

3. Draw a half note DOWN from the given note to make a WHOLE STEP. Add a sharp or a flat if indicated in the square below. Turn the stems UP in the treble clef, DOWN in the bass clef.

4. Write the name of each note in the square below it.

Connect-the-Dots Puzzle
(Whole Steps)

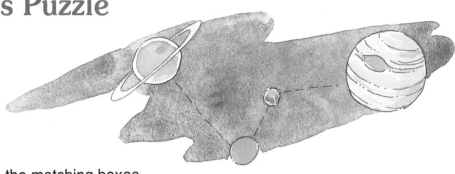

Draw lines connecting the dots on the matching boxes.

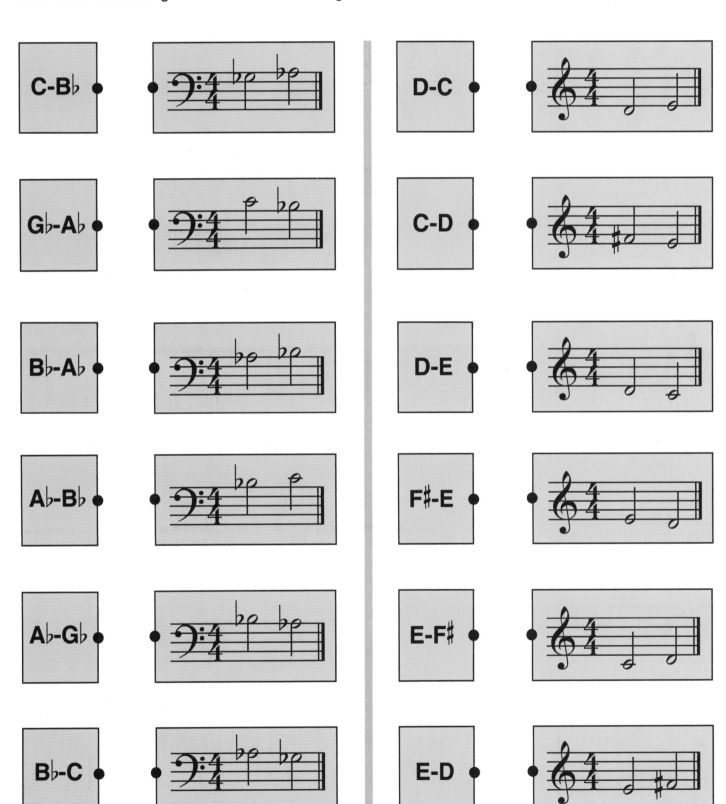

Use with pages 32–33.

Coloring Half Steps and Whole Steps

1. Color the keys on the keyboard GREEN for the half steps.
2. Color the keys on the keyboard RED for the whole steps.

 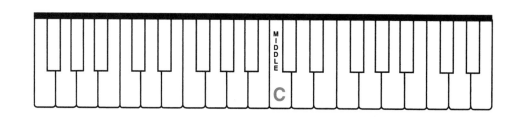

 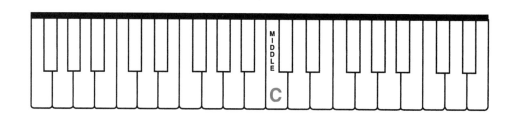

 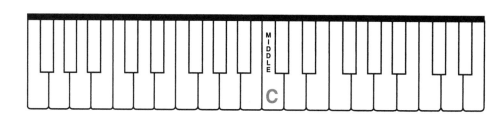

 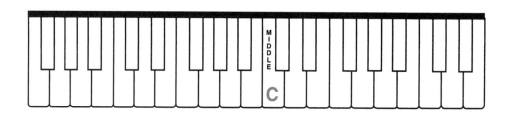

 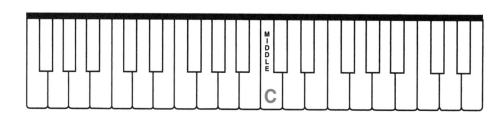

Name the Notes

Write the name of each note in the square below it—
then play and say the note names.

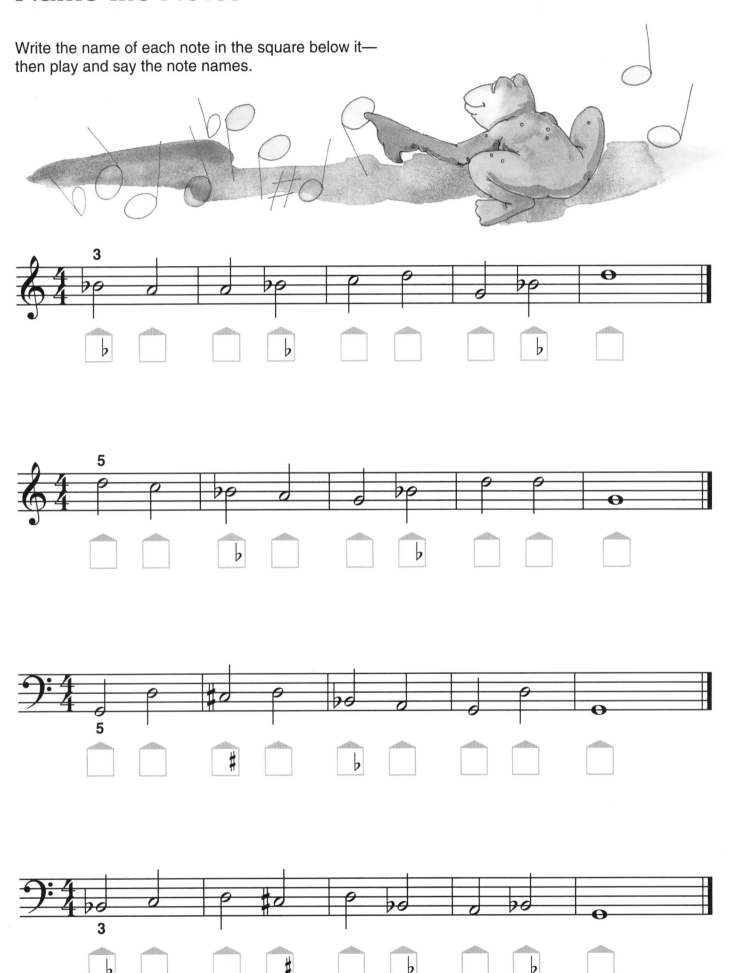

Tetrachord Match-Up

Use with page 36.

Circle the notes that match each tetrachord.

1.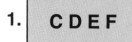

2. G A B C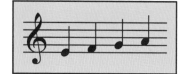

3. D E F♯ G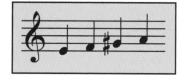

4. C D E F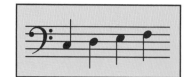

5. G A B C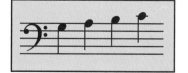

6. D E F♯ G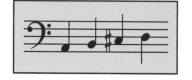

Writing the C Major Scale

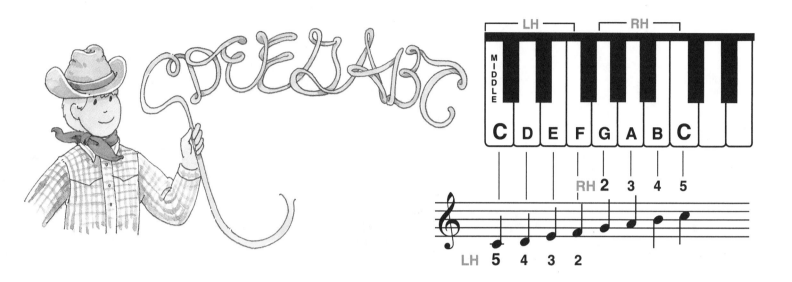

1. Write the notes of the C MAJOR SCALE in the TREBLE staff under the squares.
   Use WHOLE NOTES.

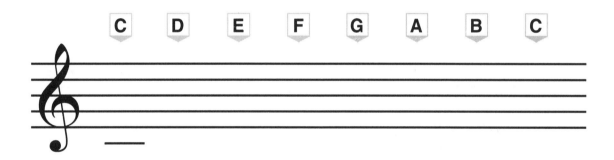

| C | D | E | F | G | A | B | C |

2. Write notes from the C MAJOR SCALE that spell these words in TREBLE CLEF.
   Use WHOLE NOTES.

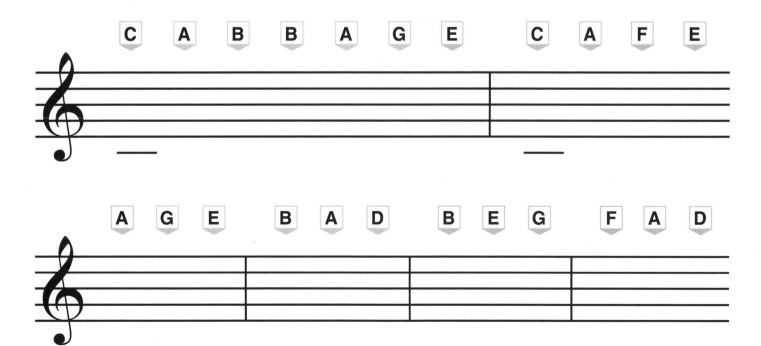

| C | A | B | B | A | G | E | | C | A | F | E |

| A | G | E | | B | A | D | | B | E | G | | F | A | D |

Use with page 37.

Writing the G Major Scale

1. Write the first four notes of the G MAJOR SCALE in the BASS staff, under the squares.
   Use WHOLE NOTES.

2. Write the last four notes of the G MAJOR SCALE in the TREBLE staff, over the squares.
   Use WHOLE NOTES.

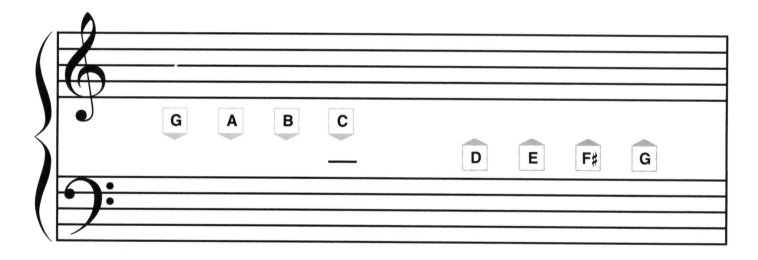

3. Write the name of each note in the square below it. The letters in each group
   of squares will spell a familiar word. Play and say the note names.

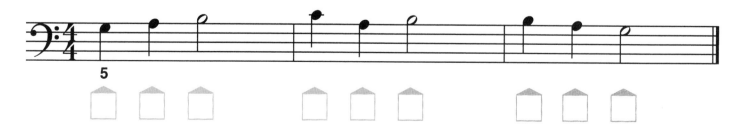

Coloring Tetrachords

1. Color the keys on the keyboard RED for notes from the C TETRACHORD.
2. Color the keys on the keyboard BLUE for notes from the G TETRACHORD.
3. Color the keys on the keyboard YELLOW for notes from the D TETRACHORD.

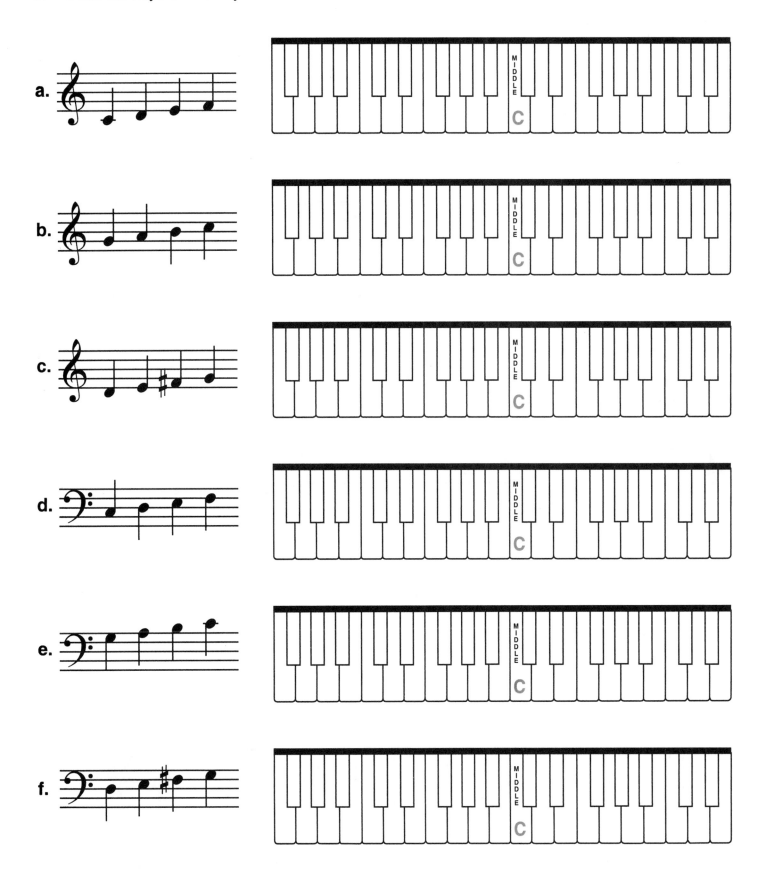

Use with pages 40–41.

Writing Missing Notes and Coloring Scales

1. Write the missing notes on the staff from the C MAJOR SCALE. Use WHOLE NOTES.

2. Write the name of each note in the square below it.

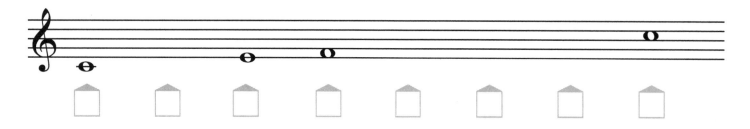

3. Color the keys on the keyboard RED for all notes in the C MAJOR SCALE written above.

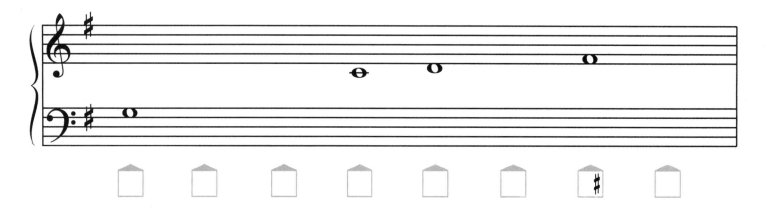

4. Write the missing notes on the staff from the G MAJOR SCALE. Use WHOLE NOTES.

5. Write the name of each note in the square below it.

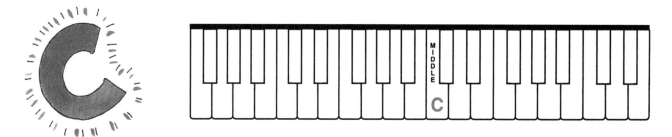

6. Color the keys on the keyboard GREEN for all notes in the G MAJOR SCALE written above.

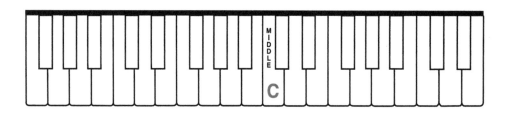

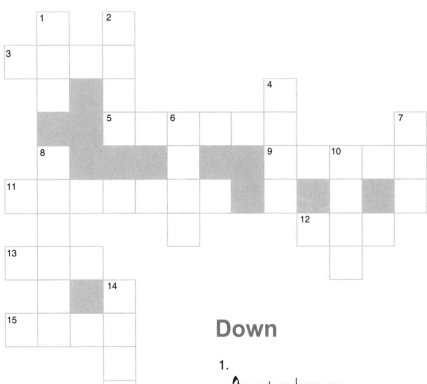

Crossword Puzzle
(Note Review)

Solve the crossword puzzle by writing
the names of the notes in the squares.

Down

1.

2.

4.

6.

7.

8.

10.

14.

16.

Across

3.

5.

9.

11.

12.

13.

15.

16.

17.

Use with pages 44–45.

Complete the Picture
(Note Review)

1. Color the areas containing an A **red**.
2. Color the areas containing a B **orange**.
3. Color the areas containing a C **purple**.
4. Color the areas containing a D **yellow**.
5. Color the areas containing an E **blue**.
6. Color the areas containing an F **pink**.
7. Color the areas containing a G **green**.

Connect-the-Dots Puzzle
(Interval Review)

1. Draw lines connecting the dots on the matching boxes.

2. Write the interval name (2, 3, 4 or 5) on the line.

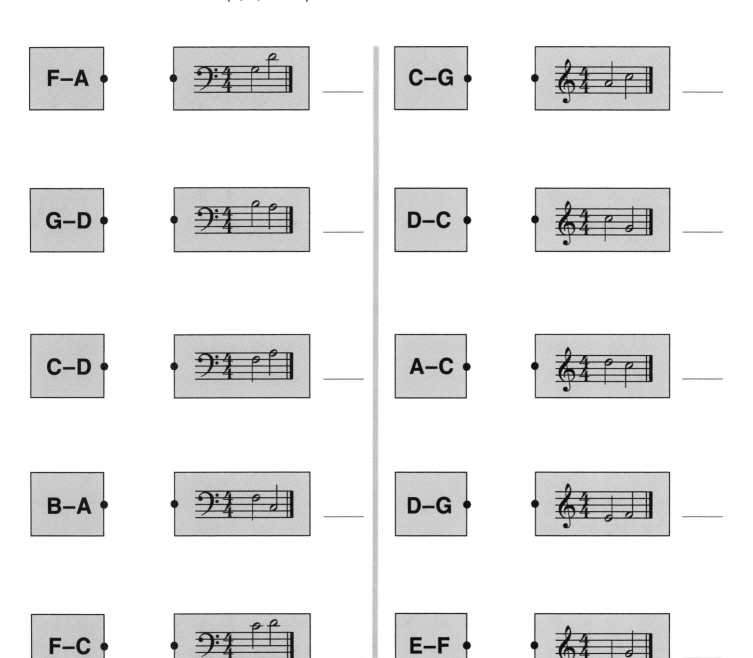

Use with pages 47–48.

Word Match-Up
(Note Review)

1. Draw lines connecting the dots on the boxes containing the word in the center column to the dots on the matching boxes in bass clef in the left column.

2. Draw lines connecting the dots on the boxes containing the word in the center column to the dots on the matching boxes in treble clef in the right column.

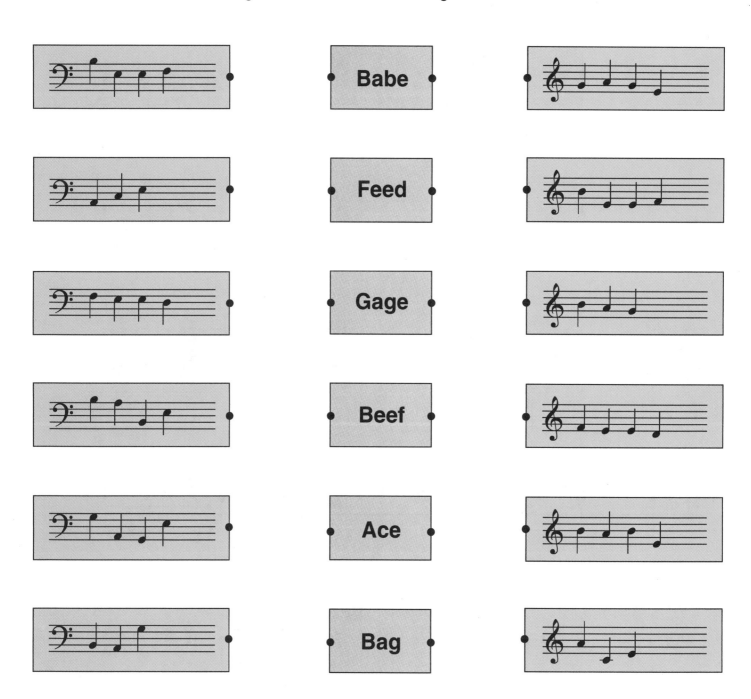